# THE GRIFFIN POETRY PRIZE
Anthology 2020

Published in Canada in 2020 and the U.S.A. in 2020 by House of Anansi Press Inc.
www.houseofanansi.com

24  23  22  21  20      1  2  3  4  5

*Library and Archives Canada Cataloguing in Publication*

Cataloguing data available from Library and Archives Canada

Cover design: Kyra Griffin and Chloé Griffin
Cover artwork: photograph by Kyra Griffin and Chloé Griffin
Inside cover photographs: A total solar eclipse taken in Libya, 2006

Canada Council
for the Arts

Conseil des Arts
du Canada

ONTARIO ARTS COUNCIL
CONSEIL DES ARTS DE L'ONTARIO
an Ontario government agency
un organisme du gouvernement de l'Ontario

*We acknowledge for their financial support of our publishing program the Canada Council
for the Arts, the Ontario Arts Council, and the Government of Canada.*

Printed and bound in Canada

# THE GRIFFIN POETRY PRIZE
## Anthology 2020

### A SELECTION OF THE SHORTLIST

Edited by HOA NGUYEN

ANANSI

PAST WINNERS AND SHORTLISTS OF
THE GRIFFIN POETRY PRIZE

## 2001

*International*
Yehuda Amichai
    Translated by Chana Bloch and
    Chana Kronfeld
**Paul Celan**
    **Translated by Nikolai Popov**
    **and Heather McHugh**
Fanny Howe
Les Murray

*Canadian*
**Anne Carson**
Ghandl of the Qayahl Llaanas
    Translated by Robert
    Bringhurst
Don McKay

## 2002

*International*
Victor Hernández Cruz
Christopher Logue
Les Murray
**Alice Notley**

*Canadian*
**Christian Bök**
Eirin Moure
Karen Solie

## 2003

*International*
Kathleen Jamie
**Paul Muldoon**
Gerald Stern
C. D. Wright

*Canadian*
**Margaret Avison**
Dionne Brand
P. K. Page

## 2004

*International*
Suji Kwock Kim
David Kirby
**August Kleinzahler**
Louis Simpson

*Canadian*
Di Brandt
Leslie Greentree
**Anne Simpson**

## 2005

| International | Canadian |
|---|---|
| Fanny Howe | **Roo Borson** |
| Michael Symmons Roberts | George Bowering |
| Matthew Rohrer | Don McKay |
| **Charles Simic** | |

## 2006

| International | Canadian |
|---|---|
| **Kamau Brathwaite** | Phil Hall |
| Durs Grünbein | **Sylvia Legris** |
| Translated by Michael | Erín Moure |
| Hofmann | |
| Michael Palmer | |
| Dunya Mikhail | |
| Translated by Elizabeth | |
| Winslow | |

## 2007

| International | Canadian |
|---|---|
| Paul Farley | Ken Babstock |
| Rodney Jones | **Don McKay** |
| Frederick Seidel | Priscila Uppal |
| **Charles Wright** | |

## 2008

| International | Canadian |
|---|---|
| **John Ashbery** | **Robin Blaser** |
| Elaine Equi | Nicole Brossard |
| César Vallejo | Translated by Robert Majzels |
| Translated by Clayton | and Erín Moure |
| Eshleman | David W. McFadden |
| David Harsent | |

## 2009

| International | Canadian |
|---|---|
| Mick Imlah | Kevin Connolly |
| Derek Mahon | Jeramy Dodds |
| **C. D. Wright** | **A. F. Moritz** |
| Dean Young | |

## 2010

| International | Canadian |
|---|---|
| John Glenday | Kate Hall |
| Louise Glück | P. K. Page |
| **Eiléan Ní Chuilleanáin** | **Karen Solie** |
| Valérie Rouzeau | |
|   Translated by Susan Wicks | |

## 2011

| International | Canadian |
|---|---|
| Seamus Heaney | **Dionne Brand** |
| Adonis | Suzanne Buffam |
|   Translated by Khaled Mattawa | John Steffler |
| François Jacqmin | |
|   Translated by Philip Mosley | |
| **Gjertrud Schnackenberg** | |

## 2012

| International | Canadian |
|---|---|
| **David Harsent** | **Ken Babstock** |
| Yusef Komunyakaa | Phil Hall |
| Sean O'Brien | Jan Zwicky |
| Tadeusz Różewicz | |
|   Translated by Joanna Trzeciak | |

## 2013

| International | Canadian |
|---|---|
| **Ghassan Zaqtan** | **David W. McFadden** |
|   **Translated by Fady Joudah** | James Pollock |
| Jennifer Maiden | Ian Williams |
| Alan Shapiro | |
| Brenda Shaughnessy | |

## 2014

| International | Canadian |
|---|---|
| Rachael Boast | **Anne Carson** |
| **Brenda Hillman** | Sue Goyette |
| Carl Phillips | Anne Michaels |
| Tomasz Różycki | |
|   Translated by Mira Rosenthal | |

## 2015

*International*
Wang Xiaoni
 Translated by Eleanor Goodman
Wioletta Greg
 Translated by Marek
 Kazmierski
**Michael Longley**
Spencer Reece

*Canadian*
Shane Book
**Jane Munro**
Russell Thornton

## 2016

*International*
**Norman Dubie**
Joy Harjo
Don Paterson
Rowan Ricardo Phillips

*Canadian*
Ulrikka S. Gernes
 Translated by Per Brask and
 Patrick Friesen
**Liz Howard**
Soraya Peerbaye

## 2017

*International*
Jane Mead
Abdellatif Laâbi
 Translated by Donald
 Nicholson-Smith
**Alice Oswald**
Denise Riley

*Canadian*
**Jordan Abel**
Hoa Nguyen
Sandra Ridley

## 2018

*International*
Tongo Eisen-Martin
**Susan Howe**
Layli Long Soldier
Natalie Shapero

*Canadian*
**Billy-Ray Belcourt**
Aisha Sasha John
Donato Mancini

## 2019

*International*
Raymond Antrobus
Daniel Borzutzky
**Kim Hyesoon**
 **Translated by Don Mee Choi**
Luljeta Lleshanaku
 Translated by Ani Gjika

*Canadian*
Dionne Brand
**Eve Joseph**
Sarah Tolmie

# CONTENTS

# PREFACE

As I start this preface, it rains and I mark two weeks in social isolation, mostly indoors with my family of four, locked into a global moment of concern. In this moment, I am brought to understand limitations, consider what has led us here, and I am reminded more than ever of interconnectivity. "All One!" reads the fresh Dr. Bronner's soap bar I use to wash my hands again.

It seems to me that we inhabit a threshold of change with challenges before us, seen and unseen. As the news evolves, as we comprehend the reach of what is yet to come, we seek ways to manage and endure as a collective. Our perspectives will fundamentally shift, as certainly as astrologers speak of Saturn's return to Aquarius. A time to revolutionize structures, they say, a period that welcomes progressive inventions, reinventions.

As often happens in times of trouble, we turn to art as a site of renewal, reflection, and comfort. Art acts as a kind of elemental hearth of the mind, one that allows empathy's entry, compassion, and new perspectives. Often that art is poetry. Poetry because it is portable, memorable, and ancient, enduring beyond limits of lifespan to speak outside of time. Oracular, an ancestral song.

Poetry is a space where this fabulous invention, language, is given fullness of expression: rhythmic, sonic, contextual, intertextual, typographic, narrative playing narrative's edge. It has the capacity to connect to tendernesses and our most spacious perceptions. A poem can be experienced, be a many-sensed energy signature. A poem can reorient perspectives and provide unknown potentials.

Last year as Griffin judges, Paula Meehan, Kei Miller, and I were assigned to read 572 books of poetry in English to arrive at our decisions regarding the International and Canadian prizes. Our reading culminated in conference calls negotiating this assessment process in and as conversation. As we approached our decisions, the COVID-19 virus suddenly arrived as a global pandemic.

When I look at our 2020 Griffin Prize selections, I reflect on how it assembles work that attests to poetry's scope and possibilities. Here, in the anthology you hold, sampled from our shortlist, you will encounter poetry in its capacity to enfold the collective inside of the singular. Poetry collaborates with language as it responds, plays, and inquires. Poetry moves with manifold meanings and associations. Poetry is past and futurity in exchange, "the real" attached to words, not as a monument to itself, but as something else, something that feels relational: a form of listening and elaboration.

Here is another short list, drawn from my editorial notes:

Poems memorate
Poems of the world between worlds
Poems in dialogue with time
Poems undercurrent
Poems of mythic place
Poems that define and redefine spatial relationships
Poems polyphony and poems palimpsest
Poems plaintive and demotic
Poems hybrid
Poems inhabit history
Poems of the numinous
Poems interacting with archive
Poems of continuing

I write this during a time of social isolation, distancing, and disinfectant and yet I consider the relationality and connective creativity that is poetry. Perhaps it is just this potentiality that I most value.

With gratitude and thanks to my fellow judges and for the immense efforts and generosity supporting the Griffin Trust for Excellence in Poetry. What incredible company. What an honour it is to introduce these poems to you, Dear Reader . . .

Hoa Nguyen, Toronto, March 2020

# THE GRIFFIN POETRY PRIZE
Anthology 2020

INTERNATIONAL
SHORTLIST

# ABIGAIL CHABITNOY

## *How to Dress a Fish*

Bringing languagelessness into language, Abigail Chabitnoy's *How to Dress a Fish* is an act of remythologizing and personal recollection, a text of redress to the violence of U.S. colonialism. Like the contronym cleave, like swallowed fish that appear whole, her poems assemble a narrative of displacement and emergence, of that which is half-revived and half-buried, to address instability and unify across divides. With gestures of archival investigation and assemblage, the poems move with undercurrent, sections, elision, and invention into voicings of self, land, story, and mythic place. "One face is not enough / to adapt / to survive / to be both predator and prey / and a shark is after all / not so different." *How to Dress a Fish* speaks of division's expression and history's fracturing violence. This is a mending inquiry.

## Family Ghosts

Michael I wrote you
a story   I didn't know
what you did
what we did
if I should dig
you up          but
it didn't feel right
you should remain so far
from the sea
it didn't feel right
I couldn't see you

Is this the shape these things should take?

*What if we were the fish?*

"In appearance, Chabitnoy's claims of being a full blooded ~~Indian~~ are fully substantiated."

*Today I learned I'm biracial. or mixed racial. ambiguously ethnic. I read it in a book, but I don't feel comfortable with any of these. Genocide elementary by comparison. Anybody can be outraged at a wrongful death. But wrongful living? I was comforted by the half white, half Mexican boy glowing beside me. Everyone wants to see ghosts, in theory.*

9

*That is to say, I still don't know how to fit this skin. I, too, am tall and well built*
*and in summer possess a strikingly characteristic face. And if I only run*
*a short distance, you can hardly tell the trouble with my back,*
*the fragmented bone attached by gristle, or not, or*
*floating just below the skin—*

Did you make yourself wind to make up your size? – *How else is a fish*
*accustomed to keeping its feet on the ground?* – Why did you come
back? Did you forget which way the wind blowed?

One summer evening Mike Chabitnoy
and some boys killed a shark
off Wood Island Coast
and dragged the beast ashore.

(the other Mike,
the son,
the one who stayed
with our aunt)

One of them jumped on the thickest part
and out flew a large salmon
from its open mouth.

Another and another until
five large perfect fish leaped forth
amid screams from the children.

*Were you*
*a shark*
*or something smaller?*

They named the shark Jonah.

"Among the many visitors here last Sunday was Michael Chabitnoy who is working at Hershey, Pa., for the summer. 'Mike' is also trying out for the Hershey baseball team."

Conduct: *good*

Why did you leave and then come back? Did you play with Jim Thorpe in school 'Mike'? Did you eat pork and milk and green beans and butter? Did you live in the Athletes' Quarters? Which tale are we in again Michael? Who gets to be of-the-water? *Who gets to be people? above or below the sea –*

*Isn't a shark just a fish after all?*

*It was winter. I was sweating. You and I were in a boat, going back to Unalaska and my body went cold to spite my discomfort. You can be wind. You can be feathers. You can be fur or fin and teeth. I am not even earth. Not even bone. But permafrost in a warming state. Cold, not cold enough. Porous. Full of holes. Not filled but*

*disappearing.*

Find a place you feel comfortable and do it.
Purse your lips together    teeth parted    tongue
holding the weight of the roof
your mouth. Inhale

                        release.


Find a place you feel comfortable with ghosts.

Rumor has it you might wake spirits
this way    this talking
how the dead talk    not in word

                        but sound.

That's not how the one from the water
survived.

How could she survive
in a box?        in pieces?

Good Friday the waters came.

On the roof she found a woman
dying with potted plants
rotting in the over-salted air.

A hole opened up in the sky if she could just reach
this sky she could reach
the ground she needed

But she needed that neck to get through.
She needed that woman's neck.

She needed a medium
of authority
of consumption or
birthing or
a way to breathe otherwise.

She needed a neck
with a mouth.

# SHARON OLDS

## *Arias*

The aria is a melody for single voice, and these poems
sing the music of what happens in the everyday with
mother, father, lover, child, unknown citizen. Memory
is elevated onto some plane of eternity by the pure lyric
grace of this work, this witness. And work it is — there
is the heft of heavy lifting, of difficult emotional materi-
al moving like magma under enormous pressure to issue
volcanically, irrupting into the moment of the poem. It
is not just that the personal is political, the intimate here
is revolutionary. If there is elegy, there is also transform-
ative empathy and an authoritative moral force. Like
Dickinson, like Whitman, like Snyder, like Rich, hers
is a voice, demotic and mythic, that defines our times.

## My Father's Whiteness

It takes me a lifetime to see my father
as a white man – to see his whiteness
(named by white men after gleaming and brightness).
I saw the muck sweat of his pallor, he'd be
faceup on the couch like a mushroom in a mushroom-forcer,
and I didn't even wonder what it would feel like
for a person to be proud of their father.
I knew that at the interfraternity council
he'd been the handsome, wisecracking one, the
president, proud he could not read,
he could always get someone to do that for him –
he liked to say the two people allowed
to graduate from his college without knowing how to
read or write were him and Herbert Hoover.
Nor did any frat house there
house a brother.
Nor did I see my father – that in order to pass
out every night on the couch, snore
and snort and gargle-sing from his chintz
sty, he had to overcome
every privilege known to a man
tall, dark, handsome, white,
straight, middle class. He had to put his
every advantage down on the street and drive
over it with that thump a tire
and a body make. O say can you see him as I
see him now, as if he had no one
to answer to, he so prepared
to devour and excrete the hopes he'd been handed
on a platter, the spoon in his mouth, he could eat
what he had not earned, he could do it in his sleep.

## Hyacinth Aria

When my mother was felled, by the sudden blow
of a stroke, decked by a deep bleed when the old
brain tumor broke through, and I flew
to her, and sang to her for the rest
of her life, for two days, sang her
out, they told my students where I had
been, and there on the seminar table
was a garden, in a small shoebox
crate, with a lattice wooden fence, in-
side it the spears of hyacinths.
This morning I leaned over her cut-glass bowl so
cut it looks about to draw blood,
and there in the water jellied with peeling
bulb-skin, down inside the thighs of the shoots, there was a
cunning jumble of bumps, rinds,
green mother grinds of hyacinths
soon to bulge, and rise, and open,
and, for a moment, I almost mourned
my mother – mourned her when she was a child,
a frail being like an insect, with papery
wings, with little, veined skirts,
before she had pummeled anyone,
before she had taken the cudgel from her own
mother to wield it in turn on me who would
take it in turn as my purple stylus,
my gold pen. And so, for a moment,
I loved my mother – she was my first chance,
my last chance, to love the human.

## I Cannot Say I Did Not

I cannot say I did not ask
to be born. I asked with my mother's beauty,
and her money. I asked with my father's desire
for his orgasms and for my mother's money.
I asked with the cradle my sister had grown out of.
I asked with my mother's longing for a son,
I asked with patriarchy. I asked
with the milk which would well in her breasts, needing to be
drained by a little, living pump.
l asked with my sister's hand-me-downs, lying
folded. I asked with geometry, with
origami, with swimming, with sewing, with
what my mind would thirst to learn.
Before I existed, I asked, with the love of my
children, to exist, and with the love of their children.
Did I ask with my tiny flat lungs
for a long portion of breaths? Did I ask
with the space in the ground, like a portion of breath,
where my body will rest, when it is motionless,
when its elements move back into the earth?
I asked, with everything I did not
have, to be born. And nowhere in any
of it was there meaning, there was only the asking
for being, and then the being, the turn
taken. I want to say that love
is the meaning, but I think that love may be
the means, what we ask with.

# From the Window of My Home-Town Hotel

On the lee slope of the small coastal mountain
which conceals the sun the first hour after its rising,
in the dry, steep ravines, the live
mist of the heat is seething like dust
left over from an earlier world.
A crow with a swimmer's shoulders works
the air. And a little bird flies up into a
tree and closes its wings, like a blossom
folded up into a bud again.
In the distance is a very old pine, now sparse
and frail as if hand-painted on a plate
washed for a hundred years. And the bell
in the tower, which rings the hours – the rhythm
of its intervals is known to me.
I am forgetting my mother. It well may be
some fur of her marrow is in a steep
trough of fog aslant in a gouge
of these hills – her bones were pestled in this city,
down the street from this hotel,
after her face had been rendered back
to her God. I don't sense her here.
At moments I picture my young self,
that long, narrow chin pointed like
a mosquito proboscis. She knew this place.
This is where she saw the grindings of the
femurs and ulnas breathing in the air,
and the crow's work by which it earned
its eggs, and where a songbird seemed
a flower again, and saw a tree
worn away by human eating,
and the double notes of several metals'

struck resonance waiting in what had
been them, before they were belled from the earth.
She wanted what was not there, and she saw and heard it.

## Her Birthday as Ashes in Seawater

By now, my mother has been pulled to the top
of many small waves, carried in the curve that curls
over, onto itself, and unknots,
again, into the liquid plain,
as her ions had first been gathered from appearances
and concepts. And her dividend,
her irreducible, like violet
down, thrown to the seals, starfish,
wolf spiders on the edge-of-Pacific
floor, I like to follow her
from matter into matter, my little quester,
as if she went to sea in a pea-green
boat. Every separate bit,
every crystal shard, seems to
be here – her nature unknowable, dense,
dispersed, her atomization a miracle,
the earth without her a miracle
as if I had arrived on my own
with nothing to owe, nothing to grieve,
nothing to fear, it would happen with me
as it would, not one molecule
lost or sent to the School Principal
or held in a dried-orange-pomander strongbox
stuck with the iron-matron maces
of the cloves. My mother is a native of this place,
she is made of the rosy plates of the shell
of one who in the silt of a trench plays
music on its own arm, draws
chords, and then the single note –
rosin, jade, blood, catgut,
siren-gut, hair, hair,

hair – I miss her, I lack my mother, such
peace there is on earth now every
tooth of her head is safe, ground down
to filaments of rock-crab fractals
and claw facets, the whole color wheel
burst and released. Oh Mom. Come sit
with me at this stone table at the bottom
of the Bay, here is a barnacle of
egg custard, here is your tiny
spoon with your initials, sup with me
at dawn on your first day – we are all
the dead, I am not apart from you,
for long, except for breath, except for
everything.

## When You Were First Visible

When you were first visible to me,
you were upside down, not sound asleep but
before sleep, blue-gray,
tethered to the other world
which followed you out from inside me. Then you
opened your silent mouth, and the first
sound, a crackling of oxygen snapping
threads of mucus, broke the quiet,
and with that gasp you pulled your first
earth
air
in, to your lungs which had been
waiting entirely compressed, the lining
touching itself all over, all inner – now each
lung became a working hollow, blown
partway full, then wholly full, the
birth day of your delicate bellows.
And then – first your face, small tragic
mask, then your slender body, flushed
a just-before-sunrise rose, and your folded,
crowded, apricot arms and legs
sprang out,
in slow blossom.
And they washed you – her, you, her –
leaving the spring cheese vernix, and they wrapped her in a
clean, not new, blanket, a child of
New York City,
and the next morning, the milk came in,
it drove the fire yarn of its food through
passageways which had passed nothing
before, now lax, slack, gushing

when she sucked, or mewled. In a month's time,
she was plump with butterfat, her wrists
invisible down somewhere inside
the richness of her flesh. My life as I had known it
had ended, my life was hers, now,
and I did not yet know her. And that was my new
life, to learn her, as much as I could,
each day, and slowly I have come to know her,
and thus myself, and all of us, and I will
not be done with my learning when I return to where she
      came from.

# SARAH RIGGS

## TRANSLATED FROM THE FRENCH WRITTEN BY ETEL ADNAN

*Time*

"I say that I'm not afraid / of dying because I haven't / yet had the experience / of death," writes Etel Adnan in the opening poem to *Time*. What is astonishing here is how she manages to give weariness its own relentless energy. We are pulled quickly through this collection — each poem, only a breath, a small measure of the time that Adnan is counting. Every breath is considered, measured, observant — perceiving even "a crack in the / texture of the day." If Adnan is correct and "writing comes from a dialogue / with time" then this is a conversation the world should be leaning into, listening to a writer who has earned every right to be listened to.

*from* **October 27, 2003**

in order to perform, words dress in
Phoenician purple, and it's in the
spaces separating them that
great adventures take place

I plunge my hands into the sun
whereas sleeping bodies prefer
slivers of the moon

let's stay in the Mediterranean, not far
from the fields planted with orange trees
in bloom

those who cannot leave
discover the geography
of the body. there are also airfields
and harbors on the surface of our souls

don't leave the Mediterranean
without telling her that you loved her:
her daughters and her sons went
North, a day of rain, or a day
of war

as for me, I belong to the stones
thrown for lack of helicopters,
to the women locked up,
to the political prisoners;
sometimes I regret my love of
splendor

but our solar mother star,
and the lunar father, in their way,
have entrusted us with useless
objects from a forgotten century

in the water of certain rivers there
is a wild happiness

in Yosemite Valley,
with the color of the Pacific still
trailing in my eyes, I buried
the essential and the inessential. That
happiness will survive my death

my friend Khaled sends me palm tree
postcards because he knows that
Europe is covered in burned petrol

I pass by the trees of this
season as I pass by
men and women . . . I believe it's
possible to have loved only
shadows

I return to Greece, preferred friend of
celestial Arabia, because they have
horses in common, and wild teenagers

I close the shutters and I wonder
where the light went that married
the sea beneath our eyes

I'd have liked to go to the corner
cafe, to watch the cold file by while I'm
in the warm, or even to make love . . .
but bombs are raining down on Baghdad

this evening, my friends, I'm going to bed
early because the dark is too thick. I'll try,
contrary to what's usual in dreams, not to let
myself be carried by waves, nor hunt
for my key. I'm going to try to sleep,
I believe, as children do

there's a time in autumn when the
trees change their nature, and
wake up beyond
matter; then one sees them come back to
their ordinary selves

*from* **No Sky**

II


In the proximity of love,
    dispersion,
    refraction,
time no longer measures itself
    against the body . . .
there is blood
    on certain roads
    and the perverse friendship of
    death

There is noise in our
hearts
an imperfect breathing
attached to ligaments:
    dull pain in the
    wrists
    and the folds

Describe the body
    if you can
and you will see how unlikely
your soul is

matter being our
    sole possession

Like the half-light where
the Pacific sleeps,
its solitude is made of gray
forms    it looks for its metaphors
in electronics, it only lives
in the pallor of signs

She, in the rose-colored song
of a bedroom, a deserted
love, and the lost time
of trees . . .

                    at
the edge of the jungle
        don't enter the
        sacred element of the present

Time has burned
that's why in the
naked lightness of the clouds
we are held back by the
nocturnal voyage

III

There remain
the folds in the slacks
the curled eyelashes
and the vigor of the
muscles:  he is
    dead

A clamp found
in a pasture,
. . . a horse stumbles

I am not
the touchstone
of the sky nor blood
circulating. At the bottom of the pages,
signatures sleep

Light in free fall
sounds like a stream
which is the language of
matter

Truths are
department stores:
you are going up,
you take the escalator,
you don't come back

In the tentative
darkness of the
raisins there was
half of the
        sun
then the shadow
of the past

Sometimes I get ready for the
    voyage of no return,
but dawn raises the curtains,
    and my adolescence
    is standing at the corner
        of nowhere

Under the wonder of
cold skies

*from* **Baalbeck**

25

The olive tree in Delphi,
next to the temple of Sikiyon,
remembers the oracle
saying that
somewhere in the plain linking
the Red Sea to the Dead Sea,
music will
displace the sky.

26

Ruins are relics.
The lineage being of little importance, we're related to
 them.

# NATALIE SCENTERS-ZAPICO

## *Lima :: Limón*

There is a driving, deliberate, righteous indignation to *Lima :: Limón*, a force that that will unsettle many readers though it is tempered with a mature and forgiving undersong of empathy and love. Natalie Scenters-Zapico is a *fronteriza*, a frontier dweller, a woman shaped by the contending cultures of Mexico and the U.S. Her unflinching gaze is turned on machismo and marianismo, and the quotidian reality of community in crisis, in an elegant poetry that speaks through masks both sacred and profane. The shadow of femicide is never far, but the poet finds a redemptive magic in the voices of the mutilated, in the traditions of ancestors, in the salvific powers of language, in poems pushed to the very edge of what can be said.

## He Has an Oral Fixation

He can't stop putting the dead
flowers, the dead-head nails, the dead weight
sacks of flour, in his mouth. He can't
stop writing about the mouth. The way

he woke up to his mouth full of bees,
their dead crunch still stinging
his gums. He writes: *There's something
beautiful in the way a mouth can be broken*

*by saliva & cold air.* She broke
his mouth open & filled it with lead-
tainted earth. She made him
brain-dead through the mouth;

licked the honey she pulled
from his incisors like sap from a tree.
His mouth, with its stretch marks
running along each cheek—she's never seen

anything like it. His mouth a scar
of his hunger, a scar of his gluttony
after the hunger. Stop writing
about the mouth: the teeth, the gums,

the impacted tooth & its psychedelic
blues & greens. Stop writing how she bit
your mouth & with a blowtorch
welded its dark-open shut. Stop writing

about the mouth: the tongue, the holy
molars, the wear of grinding yourself
to bone. Stop writing about the mouth:
his mouth, your mouth, her mouth.

## I Didn't Know You Could Buy

something not for sale until
I walked through Coyoacán
& watched gringos ignore

sign after sign: Casa No En Venta.
Still I watched men knock
on door after door stalking

houses they could paint blue,
just like Frida Kahlo's. It's like
the time two thieves knocked me

to my knees for twenty dollars.
I thought the thieves jewelers
as they punched my jaw until

each tooth turned dark amber.
Later, to save my body, I set
my teeth, muddy stones, into a crown

I wore the rest of summer. I know
how to hide bruises so the earth
won't get jealous of lightning

produced by simple friction.
My landscape of curves & edges
that breaks light spectral

is not for sale, but men still knock
on rib after rib, stalking the perfect house—
the perfect shade of blue.

## She Is à la Mode

A sheet cake soaked in milk & left suspended. She had no decorations, so she placed a sugar bowl on top. She placed her man at the head of the cake & told him to close his eyes & relax: *Lean back, mi rey, you deserve comfort at the head of my cake.* She wanted to capture the cake before it was consumed, so she called her brother-in-law & asked him to stand behind the cake for good balance. She jumped on top of the cake, folded her legs like Minnie Mouse & told everyone to be cool, this cake was going to be in a movie. She was going to call it À la Mode & this was to be the opening scene. *But there's no ice cream,* her man said. *No, my body is the ice cream,* she said & pursed her lips for the camera until her mouth became a dark wound. Her man, who adored her again for a minute, said: *You're so dumb, clean up this kitchen already, da asco.* She waited for the hot water to run & poured a cap full of bleach in the sink. She cried: *All my movies are no movies. All my movies are not mine.*

## Ixmiquilpan, Hidalgo, México

1

Part of the simulation is not knowing
your coyote's real name. Part of the simulation
is knowing your group could leave you
behind. Part of the simulation is knowing
that if you are left behind, a pickup truck
will take you back to your hotel.


2

Through caves, through brush, through needles
we form a line by holding on
to a stranger's backpack. In the dark live
rounds are fired. I duck, people laugh.


3

The desert here is no desert at all & I think of how
I could cut a thick barrel cactus open
& eat it. In Chihuahua I've never seen
thick barrel cactus, only the thin long threads
of ocotillo that don't carry much water.


4

The chairos pay 250 pesos to walk
all night in the desert in the middle of México
to simulate a border crossing. They bring jugs
filled with water & pose for selfies.

5

When you wade across the river you only have to worry
about swimming if a current pulls you under, not the red
glare of night-vision goggles, floodlights & guns.


6

In the simulation, only two people make it
to *the other side* without getting stopped by actors
portraying la migra or narcos. All are brought back
for cups of atole. *It's three in the morning*, a girl laughs.


7

I walk back to my room, turn on the light
& the flying ants won't stop swarming. It is so dark
& I have so much water left in my jug.
My teeth full of grit from the atole.

## Marianismo

For Julio Cortázar, Ana Castillo & those who know

+

A shell of teeth,
mother-of-pearl brilliant.
I wash each tooth by hand.
They are the bones
of my daughter still
to fall. A foam collects
in the vitals of the earth
full of teeth. Bones,
from my womb
washed clean with hot
water in a brass tub
& poured beneath
the ocotillo to be burned.

++

Dios te salve, María,
llena eres de gracia,
el Señor es contigo.
Bendita tu eres
entre todas las mujeres
y bendito es el fruto
de tu vientre, Jesús.
Santa María,
Madre de Dios,
ruega por nosotros
pecadores ahora
y en la hora
de nuestra muerte.

+++

No llores, María,
tell no one
of the child. Tell
no one, María,
even when machos
laugh as you hum
to yourself over
the pot of laundry.
Beat each sheet
against stone.
The washing
machine, gone
to rust in the yard.

++++

Que te salves,
María, llena eres
de rajas, estás
sola en este mundo.
Bendito es El entre
todas las mujeres
y bendito es el trabajo
de tu vientre, Jesús.
María, ama de casas,
ruega por nosotros
pecadores ahora y
en la hora de
nuestro nacimiento.

+++++

María, when your macho
comes knocking at the back
gate, turn each light
off. Pretend no one
is home, María. Pretend
you are not home, in your
body. Pretend your body
did not lose pressed
skin & blood. Pretend
you did not rid yourself
of your child, of your
baby, by your body,
your cuerpo. Your body?

++++++

The desert is always
hungry. I break
rock to dirt
with a pick. Sky
breaks in shards.
I wash the child, hope
to hear a scream.
She is dead, but I
carry her, eyes closed,
through the yard &
breathe into her
mouth, which looks
like my mouth.

+++++++

Who is the father,
Maria? Does it matter
who it was if he
isn't here now?
Does it matter who
it was if he wasn't
here when from
between your legs
you bled into bedding
onto the floor. You made
this baby, it was your
baby. You made it,
it was yours.

++++++++

There is no damp earth
here, only powder
I grind from teeth
to use as dye for thread.
This is my solitary
burial. No macho cares
for the child born but not
breathing. My baby, I tried
to roll myself into a ball
as he kicked to break
teeth, but you would not
stop bleeding, you kept
flooding between my knees.

+++++++++

Dios te dejo,
María, llena eres de
llantos, el Señor
te dejo en el desierto.
Bendita es tu hija,
muerta debajo del
ocotillo, y bendita
es su flor, roja como
le sangre que florece.
Santa María, madre
de la hija muerta
antes de vivir,
ruega, ruega, ruega.

## Buen Esqueleto

Life is short & I tell this to mis hijas.
Life is short & I show them how to talk
to police without opening the door, how
to leave the social security number blank
on the exam, I tell this to mis hijas.
This world tells them I hate you every day
& I don't keep this from mis hijas
because of the bus driver who kicks them out
onto the street for fare evasion. Because I love
mis hijas, I keep them from men who'd knock
their heads together just to hear the chime.
Life is short & the world is terrible. I know
no kind strangers in this country who aren't
sisters a desert away & I don't keep this
from mis hijas. It's not my job to sell
them the world, but to keep them safe
in case I get deported. Our first
landlord said with a bucket of bleach
the mold would come right off. He shook
mis hijas, said they had good bones
for hard work. *Mi'jas, could we make this place
beautiful?* I tried to make this place beautiful.

CANADIAN

SHORTLIST

# CHANTAL GIBSON

## *How She Read*

Chantal Gibson invites scrutiny of where language maps, or fails to map, the quiddity of the world. Here the English language carries and transmits the burden of its service to the imperial "adventure," in schoolbooks, in literature, in historical artifacts, and through image and portraiture in paint and photograph. Her interanimation of the visual and the verbal energizes a private mark-making, a resistance poetry to the coded, at times subliminal, oppressions of history. To detox the soul then, to be free and creative as citizens, we deserve to read each mark with schooled attention. And trust in our own mark making, our right to speak it the way we see it. This is a fabulous primer, ludic and ferocious, in the grand tradition of liberation handbooks.

## homographs

1: a race with skin
pigmentation different
from the white
race (esp. Blacks);

You preferred *coloured* back then, stung less than
*negro*. *Mulatto* is dated. I'm *mixed race* now.

2: complexion tint,
a characteristic of
good health;

No one noticed the colour in your cheeks. The
Christmas dinner one-liner, "Must've been dirty,
it even made *you* blush!" At least you taught me
how to take a joke.

3: of interest, variety,
and intensity;

Remember Cabbagetown? Our coloured
beginnings, the dress shop lady, the front door,
my broken pointy finger, you in your secretary
dress chasing her in the street. *Girl*, where you
learn to fight like that?

4: to give a deceptive
explanation or excuse
for;

The lawyer argued you were coloured by your
emotions. Quite naturally, of course. What other
reason would you have to beat a white bitch
down?

5: to modify or bias;

My world, coloured. Never has a child felt more
loved, more protected, more ashamed.

6: an outward or token
appearance or form that is
deliberately misleading;

You coloured your apology with the single
mother story of my one good eye. The white lady
dropped the charges.

7: of character, nature;

You said, *Wait long enough, you'll see their true colours.*
I never told you she smiled at me as she turned
away, or that I stuck my finger in the hinge just to
see what would happen.

## homonyms


You said, *Hand me that knife, girl, handle first.*
I whispered ⟍ ⟋ ⟍ into my sorry-looking finger-
nails, prayed you could make Nana's pastry from
scratch, keep that shiny blade away from your skin,
and stop the chemo shakes enough to cut 1 finger

of shortening into 4 cups of flour. We knead our
fingers in a little egg and water to hold it together.
We need our hands to touch and turn this mixing
bowl into a talisman. *Jus skin n bones, girl,* you wink
an elbow into my ribs, pray there's time to make

a woman of me, but you just scratch the surface of
my adolescence. If I'd stop biting my nails, stand up
straight, we wouldn't have to fight tooth n nail to get
along. You play "Stuck on You" for the umpteenth time,
snap your fingers on the downbeat. I count (5, 6, 7,

and 8) every scratch on the vinyl, mutter something
foolish like, *Wish you'd keep your hands off my stuff,*
til your backhand reminds me I am your stuff, always
under your skin, eyes rolling, all sass n backtalk, til
you're itchin to skin me alive. I can't stop counting

down the days til I graduate and nail down a real job.
I'm so full of straight As, you can't praise me or beat me
down. You're too tired to raise a finger and say, *Don't
ever let a man lay a hand on you, girl.* You just ⟍ ⟋ ⟍ ,
pass the rolling pin and scratch me off your to do list.

Nana says you damn near scratched the black off, flesh
down to the bone. The white coats took years to nail
down a diagnosis, Hodgkin's, not hysteria, wearing away
your fingertips. When Lionel hit No. 1, you didn't have
a prayer. Nor did I really, an unfinished woman, stuck

on you, praying for second chances, a white-knuckled
life, the surface slightly scratched. I remember to untuck
my thumbs to avoid snapping my fingers whenever I get
the nerve to throw a punch. The white coat says I'll be fine.
If you were here, would you paint my nails or nurse me

with the back of your hand?

## An Introduction to Cultural Studies (for EJ)

You used to sit with me while I'd take a bath, til
you were about eleven, chat and count the Avon
bath beads you gave me for Christmas. I doubt
it ever occurred to you that a woman with three
kids might want a little time alone. For a while,

you'd always bring some book or magazine,
Judy Blume, Nancy Drew, some *Teen Beat*,
*Tiger Beat* foolishness with white boys on it,
the *Toronto Star*, the Sears catalogue, a *World
Book Encyclopedia*—but, you wouldn't read

them to me, you'd just tell me about what you'd
learned, if you liked them or not—always white
pieces of blue-lined three-ring binder paper torn
and placed between the pages you prepared to
discuss. When you preferred that Shaun Cassidy

over his brother, David, I asked what coloured
boys did you like, but you couldn't think of any,
except for Michael Jackson. But you didn't like
him in *that way*. When the Beatles invaded in
'64, I didn't like Sam Cooke in that way, either.

I remember '77, the summer of Emanuel Jaques,
The Shoeshine Boy found dead on a rooftop in a
garbage bag. I nearly wept when you asked me
about Yonge St., faggots, body rubs, as if I'd know
*how* those child raping degenerates could drown

a young boy in a sink. You Scotch-taped the *Star*
clippings in saran wrap, careful to keep them dry.
When you said, *Mom, only poor kids get lured away
and snatched in bags*, I understood your insistence
and stopped reading your sisters *Curious George*.

Sometimes, I'd watch you watching me, your gaze:
water beads in my fro, my big boobs floating in the
fake-lavender-scented water, my pink C-section scar,
the wiry hair between my legs, like you were trying
to figure me out, like you were trying to see the future.

# Mountain Pine Beetle Suite

## I. dendroctonus ponderosae

They come with axes between their teeth. Pioneer beetles,
females hungry for trees, ready to carve an instant town    out

of the wilderness. Somewhere in the needling green sprawl
between Darwin & God, an edict etched deep & tingling

beneath the skin, they believe *this* stand of old pines will last
a lifetime. By nature, they desire. A species wants

nothing more than to procreate. Back home,
a pheromone frenzy stirs a gnashing appetite

for industry. The new believers wake & uncross
their legs, hell-bent on leaving this unholy land

of hollow trees. How soon they forget the splinter's prick
between their lips. In unison, they hum, the blue-

stained settlers, young males itching to leave this once-
Eden girdled & snap-necked. A ghost town rusting, their dead

pitched out of the trees. Meanwhile the humans look
petrified, like butterflies shocked in resin, arms wide,

palms flat against the front room window, disbelieving
the *FOR SALE* sign on the lawn, wishing away

the dust on the toys piled up in the driveway.

## II. summer: mating season

the female plays house  between
the bark & the sapwood  she is
hard-wired for love  in the phloem
her scent on the walls   she rubs
her Avon wrists together  & waits

the male finds her intoxicated  they
make love  under the trees  legs be-
come arms  hands grow fingers  nails
scratch  tiny love notes  in the bark

summer is short here  little time
for courtship in the North:  the cold-
blooded retreat to the woods   veins
pumped with antifreeze  the female
bores deeper  into the sapwood  she
drags her smokes  & her big belly  up
the tree  carves her birthing chamber
and her coffin with her teeth

### III. homo sapiens

Girl, there's a red stain on your floral dress
trying hard to look like a rose.  Usually

you don't bleed this much.
It just takes a minute to stop:

a dab of Vaseline, a greasy piece
of rolled up toilet paper shoved up

your nose, the tissue bent
and twisted a few times

to reach the broken blood vessels.
In the back of your mind, you know

you'll have to see the doc, probably
have it cauterized. Tell him it was just

an accident, no need to fill out a report (no
big deal).  It's a small town, after all.

Everyone talks.  But no one told you
*it* would look like this, marriage:

your high school sweetheart, a sawmill job,
a house, two kids, a camper, a truck,

and a severance check.
You borrowed

your mother's fairy tale, a ponytail dream
you can get with a Grade 12 diploma.

It all started with a forest and a knife
and an old pine tree with your name on it.

Remember? The hands
that lit your smokes first,

that wooed the knot from your halter top
and filled the back pockets of your jeans,

that drew circles on your round belly
and caressed your pink baby scar,

have somehow forgotten
how to touch you without leaving

a mark. A little foundation and some lipstick,
and you're good as new, right? Tell the kids

you'll be out in a sec. It's time
to get ready for bed. Tuck in

your pocket an extra white tissue, just in case
the bleeding starts. *Daddy will be back soon*

*to tell you a story.* Is that what you'll say—
this time—when you open the bathroom door

and try to smile away the swelling, when you find
a kitchen chair in front of the fridge, and your 4-year-old

daughter holding out a bag of frozen peas?

## IV. obituary

wide mouth masons, shard glass, steamed
cabbage, boiling water n beets, some days
her countertops wept and the white tile floor
was a blistering purple sea

let us remember the curved lines bracketing her
parenthetical smile

sometimes she missed the 401 exit to _____ Street
and followed the broken line to Guysborough bi-
secting her fists, not long before the beetles came
and the old pines laid down their weary branches

she surrendered to Science: a needle-punctured
landscape, pretending Prince George had a coast-
line, she traded the shit stank of pulp for the scent
of Atlantic sea salt

she was a card reader, a fortune teller, a knocked-
over stop sign that said, *No one promised you a life
without corners*

she taught her daughter how to make a fist, to un-
tuck the thumb, expose it just enough to take the
impact of a punch without breaking

she giggled when he called it *croshit*, after she took
to crocheting afghans and doilies, nothing prepared
him for a widower's life of small cups of soup & half
sandwiches

she leaves behind a question mark, a flickering
light, and a northern village of bones, a peaceful scene
staged on a lake in the quiet corner of morning, as if

she has every intention
of coming back

# DOYALI ISLAM

*heft*

Laid out against the horizontal landscape of the page, from the very beginning these poems demand from the reader a reorientation, and set out a goal to teach us how to read differently — not only the poems but also the world. What is beautiful and successful here is the way Doyali Islam takes small moments and gives to them an incredible, sometimes aching, heft: the ephemera left in a pocket become a map leading us back to love; an ant observed on the floor finds its way onto a white page — a black mark effectively writing its own poem, "struggling to interpret its situation." In each of these poems, Islam makes that struggle for interpretation both wonderful and worthwhile.

**poem for your pocket**

what my pockets have kept over seasons:

coffee change. house keys. ttc tokens.
emptiness and silence and my ungloved

reticent hands. poems. thoughts of miklós
radnóti—he who hid in his pocket
a thin notebook on his forced march toward

death in some unallied forest.          forced

beyond reason to one mass grave, one mass
silence. still, one silence his overcoat

pocket would not keep: eighteen months
passed before his wife unpacked that pocket

of earth—rifled through corpses, clothing—found
what remained. it was love. love rifled through

miklós's silences—love gave his damp
last pages back to sunlight's keep. oh yes

yes, it was love announcing in him, *i*
*will find my way to you, i will come back.*

73

## visit to a thrift shop

2006

i can't remember which london corner
but i remember the brown corduroy
making something of my legs as she searched.
not purses, but knits . . . outside, winter streets
hold shuffling figures close for passing warmth.
in a mirror a face not quite hers sees
her, searching too. *when will you return?* she

turns, once again leaving, left. knows she is
already forgetting the charge of her
mother's eyes, their colour like karkade
steeped in evenings. what this language would call
*hibiscus.* she sleeps between fits and wakes
to the tv on the wall's other side.
she knows it muffles grief, and points to it.

# confronting global change

*university of toronto*

last requirement i need to graduate
so instead of komunyakaa and keats
i'm learning hadley cells, trophic states, plate
  tectonics, and the k-pg boundary.
from her lectern, professor tutty's voice
drones: *an asteroid left dinosaurs extinct.*
i scroll through world news: cement in gaza

now fifty dollars a bag—the going
rate on the black market. one man, 'imād,
has found a way to rebuild his home with sand,
gypsum, and limestone. between the clicks of
powerpoint slides, i dream seafloor shells, bones
stirring in walls: forgotten, lithified
things buzzing, buzzing beneath a drone's wings.

## the ant

i pointed to the creature on the floor:
the one hauling a burden, a rice grain;
the one who had come from a sunlit wood.
such a slight thing, to fear its composure.
my father's eyes followed my gesture through
to its visible end, and his hand placed
a cup over the fraught form. so, it traced
the perimeter of its plastic cage,
wondering at the hard unseeable edge,
hurrying to make sense of its enclosure.
his hand tore off a piece of envelope
and slid the white scrap under the cup.
then the ant was a black mark on a page,
struggling to interpret its situation,

while we spoke over it, opening a door.
so too, one day, will he be ushered out,
back into brightness in which once he stood,
a slight thing exiting a hooded world,
a smallness held close by someone like me,
the white scrap laid over, in quietude.
but before he passes that ringless gate,
tunnelling through a belt of mystery

—which is to speak of the journey of ants—

he'll have looked for a burden all his life—
something to heft, heft for nourishment;
something to pain him and free him, at once.

## moving

*1993*

squished into the back of a minivan,
my mother, my sister, and i. us three;
passenger left empty—a depression
in this landscape, vanscape; a placeholder
for *father, depressed father, my father.*
twenty-six years, and still i remember
our driver—an *ed,* an accuracy
verified by my mother, whose diary
supplies this square filipino realtor
a surname: *shosha.* at seven,
i'm not sure how to spell it, but it sounds
hushed or rustling—how the late-spring night feels
between showings, and how we move through them:
each 30 seconds, devoid of lingering.

in the minivan, ed asks my mother
what she does for a living—a question
so casual and usual he does not see
our bodies stiffen; the grand houses
we're viewing in tension with our actual
situation. *accounting,* she offers,
hiding the truth of telemarketing.
all these years
all these years
i've not once heard my mother
ask for succour, and this backseat-night we
humour her—weigh each place's merits; ours
for the choosing. through darkness—buckled, hurtling—
just for a moment, we are moving.

mondavi 1    2    burial at kobani

| | |
|---|---|
| after leaving mondavi for paris | if you must choose a burden, choose |
| camus wrote of sisyphus: | one that nourishes, drives you home: |
| *that hour like a breathing-space* | ants know this, and all who |
| *which returns as surely as his suffering,* | in longing |
| *that is the hour of consciousness* | haul the burden of love |

# daniel

soon after you were born, doctors

scraped away each blue eye. early '80s;

the practice, *emucleation*—which the ear

registers as *atomic disaster*,

though it isn't.
    & when for the first time

you removed before me the artifice,

sockets left naked, i might have turned

away, but i didn't. companions
for each other, each an imperfect

orb: acrylic, with vessels of red silk.
irides green & unmuted in their

lustre. we stood there by the bathroom sink,
passing the prostheses between us.

each bore the weight of a gold band. they fit
in our palms like two dice, a luckier hand.

# KAIE KELLOUGH

## *Magnetic Equator*

Speaking to Caribbean and hemispheric migrations, the poems in *Magnetic Equator* recall trouble, hybridity, steep falls, continuance, and elaboration. Taking on influence, place, and racialized diasporic experience as it draws language into geographic drifts and historic collisions, these are voicings that cascade and collect "an accent adrift in its second language / over a b-side version of empire." Singing of exile and scattering, the text negotiates survival and revolt as it moves with the surety and complexity of improvisation and collaboration. Sonic, visual, and intertextual, Kaie Kellough traces source and accumulation: "our crossings of past, we depart / opposite, along the sentence that encircles the world."

potararapidsfume}slide{e////////x}i{ûûûûûûûûû}l{e||||||||||||s}cascade{intothegreen

smokefallsupward}riddim{e|||||||||||||v}a{ûûûûûûûûûû}p{o\\\\\\\\r}sense{kiskadeesmist

yellowblur}ravings{a\\\\\\\\t}e{ûûûûûûûûûû}i{n////////t}bromeliads{rivershimmer

junglefrondsfurl}green{h|||||||||||||e}m{ûûûûûûûûûû}i{s|||||||||||||t}fronds{dreamsdangle

goldenfrogsstare}tropes{w////////a}f{ûûûûûûûûûû}t{i\\\\\\\\n}dread{pooleddewripples

waterthunders}unfurl{g|||||||||||||o}v{ûûûûûûûûûû}e{r////////t}voices{birdsflit&zip

lizardsfreeze}babble{h\\\\\\\\e}w{ûûûûûûûûûû}a{t|||||||||||||e}gibber{foamcascades

cacophonous}riddim{r|||||||||||||f}a{ûûûûûûûûûû}l{l\\\\\\\\g}bubbles{spiritlevel

greensphere}ravings{e////////n}e{ûûûûûûûûûû}r{a////////t}rise{arrowheadidea

timeless.creator}green{o|||||||||||||r}o{ûûûûûûûûûû}f{e|||||||||||||l}senses{earth'srockjaw

grinswidegapes}tumble{e\\\\\\\\c}t{ûûûûûûûûûû}r{i\\\\\\\\c}exiled{afarfrothingroar

envelopsvegetable}tropes{b|||||||||||||l}o{ûûûûûûûûûû}o{m////////s}froth{kingdomsound

rumblesechoes}blue{c////////r}e{ûûûûûûûûûû}o{l|||||||||||||e}distances{growth'sbustle

densitiesofpetals}solar{d|||||||||||||i}a{ûûûûûûûûûû}l{e\\\\\\\\c}gong{explodeexceed

ferntracefossil}resounds{t////////l}i{ûûûûûûûûûû}l{i|||||||||||||e}golden{leavesdecompose

dampmapforest}flower{s|||||||||||||h}o{ûûûûûûûûûû}o{t\\\\\\\\s}adrift{floorbreathingover

loverdevourer}mist{r\\\\\\\\u}s{ûûûûûûûûûû}t{e////////d}hoarse{earthomnivore

recyclescultures}roar{t|||||||||||||r}u{ûûûûûûûûûû}n{k|||||||||||||s}thrum{digestscenturies

issueslivingshoots}tropes{e////////s}c{ûûûûûûûûûû}a{p\\\\\\\\e}dread{plantrumination

orchid.heliconia}drone{m|||||||||||||a}p{ûûûûûûûûûû}m{a////////p}voice{victoriaamazonica

floweringfutures}soaked{c\\\\\\\\r}e{ûûûûûûûûûû}a{t|||||||||||||e}solar{sepalpetalpistil

stamentongue}riddim{e|||||||||||||c}h{ûûûûûûûûûû}o{e\\\\\\\\s}earth{speechdefying

empire'sseasons}ravings{e////////x}i{ûûûûûûûûûû}l{e////////s}eternal{riddymravings

bubbleonthecreole}think{c|||||||||||||o}n{ûûûûûûûûûû}t{e|||||||||||||m}vine{continuum,cook

languagesdown}syllable{p\\\\\\\\l}a{ûûûûûûûûûû}t{e\\\\\\\\s}drown{distilledsound

syllablesricochet}tropes{s|||||||||||||i}l{ûûûûûûûûûû}e{n////////t}sense{amongleavescries

curvebetween}shade{g////////e}n{ûûûûûûûûûû}e{r|||||||||||||a}tempo{solidtrunksradiate

strangegrammar}lost{t|||||||||||||i}o{ûûûûûûûûûû}n{s\\\\\\\\o}voice{bubbleatthepotaro

river'smemory}babble{f////////p}l{ûûûûûûûûûû}a{n|||||||||||||t}float{bankgurgle

anaturalhistory}naked{c|||||||||||||y}c{ûûûûûûûûûû}l{e\\\\\\\\s}sense{betweenmossslick

rockswordrides}ravings{b\\\\\\\\l}o{ûûûûûûûûûû}o{d////////i}exiled{riverripples

africvocabulary}green{n|||||||||||||t}h{ûûûûûûûûûû}e{v|||||||||||||i}afterlife{barrelsoverhoarse

falls'roar.rides}sprouts{n////////e}s{ûûûûûûûûûû}x{e\\\\\\\\e}spirit{syntacticsoar yellowblur}ravings{a\\\\\\\\t}e{ûûûûûûûûûû}i{n////////t}bromeliads{rivershimmer

junglefrondsfurl}green{h|||||||||||||e}m{ûûûûûûûûûû}i{s|||||||||||||t}fronds{dreamsdangle

goldenfrogsstare}tropes{w////////a}f{ûûûûûûûûûû}t{i\\\\\\\\n}dread{pooleddewripples

waterthunders}unfurl{g|||||||||||||o}v{ûûûûûûûûûû}e{r////////t}voices{birdsflit&zip

lizardsblink}babble{h\\\\\\\\e}w{ûûûûûûûûûû}a{t|||||||||||||e}gibber{foamcascades

cacophonous}riddim{r|||||||||||||f}a{ûûûûûûûûûû}l{l\\\\\\\\g}bubbles{spiritlevel

greensphere}ravings{e////////n}e{ûûûûûûûûûû}r{a////////t}rise{arrowheadidea

timeless.creator}green{o|||||||||||||r}o{ûûûûûûûûûû}f{e|||||||||||||l}senses{earth'srockjaw

grindswidegapes}tumble{e\\\\\\\\c}t{ûûûûûûûûûû}r{i\\\\\\\\c}exiled{afarfrothingroar

envelopsvegetable}tropes{b|||||||||||||l}o{ûûûûûûûûûû}o{m////////s}froth{kingdomsound

rumblesechoes}blue{c////////r}e{ûûûûûûûûûû}o{l|||||||||||||e}distances{growth'sbustle

empire'sseasons}ravings{e////////x}i{ûûûûûûûûûû}l{e////////s}eternal{riddymravings

bubbleonthecreole}think{c|||||||||||||o}n{ûûûûûûûûûû}t{e|||||||||||||m}vine{continuum,cook

languagesdown}syllable{p\\\\\\\\l}a{ûûûûûûûûûû}t{e\\\\\\\\s}drown{distilledsound

syllablesricochet}tropes{s|||||||||||||i}l{ûûûûûûûûûû}e{n////////t}sense{amongleavescries

curvebetween}shade{g////////e}n{ûûûûûûûûûû}e{r|||||||||||||a}tempo{solidtrunksradiate

strangegrammar}lost{t|||||||||||||i}o{ûûûûûûûûûû}n{s\\\\\\\\o}voice{bubbleatthepotaro

river'smemory}babble{f////////p}l{ûûûûûûûûûû}a{n|||||||||||||t}float{bankgurgle

potararapidsfume}slide{e////////x}i{ûûûûûûûûûû}l{e|||||||||||||s}cascade{intothegreen

smokefallsupward}riddim{e|||||||||||||v}a{ûûûûûûûûûû}p{o\\\\\\\\r}sense{kiskadeesmist

yellowblur}ravings{a\\\\\\\\t}e{ûûûûûûûûûû}i{n////////t}bromeliads{rivershimmer

junglefrondsfurl}green{h|||||||||||||e}m{ûûûûûûûûûû}i{s|||||||||||||t}fronds{dreamsdangle

goldenfrogsstare}tropes{w////////a}f{ûûûûûûûûûû}t{i\\\\\\\\n}dread{pooleddewripples

waterthunders}unfurl{g|||||||||||||o}v{ûûûûûûûûûû}e{r////////t}voices{birdsflit&zip

orchid.heliconia}drone{m|||||||||||||a}p{ûûûûûûûûûû}m{a////////p}voice{victoriaamazonica

floweringfutures}soaked{c\\\\\\\\r}e{ûûûûûûûûûû}a{t|||||||||||||e}solar{sepalpetalpistil

stamentongue}riddim{e|||||||||||||c}h{ûûûûûûûûûû}o{e\\\\\\\\s}earth{speechdefying

empire'sseasons}ravings{e////////x}i{ûûûûûûûûûû}l{e////////s}eternal{riddymravings

bubbleonthecreole}think{c|||||||||||||o}n{ûûûûûûûûûû}t{e|||||||||||||m}vine{continuum,cook

river'smemory}babble{f////////p}l{ûûûûûûûûûû}a{n|||||||||||||t}float{bankgurgle

anaturalhistory}naked{c|||||||||||||y}c{ûûûûûûûûûû}l{e\\\\\\\\s}sense{betweenmossslick

rockswordrides}ravings{b\\\\\\\\l}o{ûûûûûûûûûû}o{d////////i}exiled{riverripples

# *from* **mantra of no return**

we gear into georgetown traffic, brake across latitudes, across martin carter's
"insurgent geographies     the city's compressed cacophony     echoes
lagos, mumbai, where urgencies converge, simultaneous, improvised
     a goat roped to a post by a ditch and a man burning his trash by the
veer of the road     the schoolchildren filing out of jalousied buildings,
white starched shirts          blown sails above the oceans of navy skirts
     news radio fires: we are two weeks out from election. signs blare their colors
          yellow, green / red, black          checker as neighborhoods flutter
in glass. kokers hang     used guillotines above bled canals. the painted
houses in republic park, their electric gates and razor-wire grin
          boarded stores downtown. the humidity          the pre-election
scream          transmit, and rain's morse responds, deluges us with its
translucent code. cars pull to shoulder. wait, worry drain into the city's gullies,
one meter below sea          level. a tension: granger or ramotar, the invisible
future or the season of the present draws taut across foreheads, around mouths.
a pulse presses out at temples: who will win, the black man or the indian?
what will sprout in this racial cleft     this fusion? the words
          warble, rewind, rain
interjects, rain on the chassis

my mother occupies the passenger seat. my brother and i
        stick in the back.
    the radio babbles and sings between us. she is estranged, returning
        and we are revenants to a place            inside a narration contrived
to read like non-fiction, a continuous telling since                    one
mouth inside another, one word emigrating from another's vowels.
    a paper place we've glossed            in novels, in atlases
        materialized into sweltering road            printed under us, the car
horns blasting past, the black faces that map ours for relevance, the faces that
could belong to our relatives        faces we are instructed not to trust, into
whose night we are cautioned against venturing, whose have-not we must not
tempt. my mother banters with the river                driver, her voice
angles into        accent, some words chop        others stretch, she ent
home, but her return bends
        here, her speech            soaks into the air near the equator

*from* **zero degrees**

now that you have lain down in the back seat, the cassette clicks
and begins its slow spin, the album *exodus*. as the band sings and
soars, you sink into the silver upholstery of the oldsmobile
cutlass supreme, into the softness of the suburbs, the fuzz of
tylenol and carbon monoxide that bleaches the air in the car. the
interior is white, impenetrable with engine exhaust. you think
about what you want to write. you want to explain, but then you
don't. you want to lash out, scrawl, dismiss life as a decision
forced upon you. how do you begin. you close your eyes and
think, and the thought drips from your limp fingers. the
page        if anyone were to look in the window they would not
see the boy lolling in the back seat. the air is dense,
unbreathable, but the body still heaves. its biology drives it
to        . this is its will. it shudders as it gulps        the
music        the wailers band rides their upbeat skank, rides
their pneumatic bassline through the analog cloud, a mystic song
that stalled        breath can't silence, delivering its message
even as a shadow crowds the cranium        a high, hoarse wail
piercing the engine's numbing hum, a voice suffused with sorrow
and rage refuting sleep, scorning resignation, singing your self
up, up out of the car, out of the darkened garage and toward the
brilliance that explodes into shards and pierces pupils, stinging
you back into sunlight and leaf

the truth?
is the white cursive issued from a brick chimney
is a skeleton in brown gabardine
wandering the underground city, an accent
adrift in its second language
over a b-side version of empire
i speak french. i am a sovereign state drifter
winter hinterlander with a mortgage
and expired aeroplan points, a vacation blazing
on the credit line
unnecessary to history, my culture extracurricular
creole vernacular stutterer, i ride the metro
underground with my fur
collar tickling my chatter, metro shuttle station to station,
but i don't matter, carapace of white earbuds contains my rude—
redemption, i go to work in the heart of a conquered
devotion, a thin mist descends over me
a blown surrender,
snow falls through me. it is always snowing inside me.
my hand is a blue *fleur-de-lys* torched by autumn
my sap is slow, it hardens glistening in its circuit,
the sharpness of pine and spruce tingles
on the yellow edge of my breath
i find refuge from winter in the hudson's bay
boxing day sale. born in a corporation, i can't pretend,
i was not born on the equator,
i died in the upholstered ease of a sedan, and here is my after,
    city blistered
gray by salt and winter, work in a tower, a payment plan carrying
    anonymous
class aspirations, and this
is my squalor, an abstract longing to cruise the foothills in a
    lincoln continental
hearse, bleached teeth chattering nonsense as the zero of winter
    ascends

one tectonic plate buckled under another, mountains. i have heard my
relatives say they don't want to be buried in the cold ground     a refutation of
this place where they have wintered, years, a refutation of their own refusal
here, a double negative, a final rebuke to issue, a final no, i refuse you who
refused me, forever. stern confirmation that they must be laid to rest in the
south american soil near the turning equator. this makes sense to me. this
refusal, this remove, that they do not want this discriminating earth, that
you can't own me forever     we sealed my uncle's ashes in their bamboo urn.
after the disruptions of flight and customs, the jostling     sweating, the
rumpled linen, the searches and questions, the delays     the bewildered
eruptions, the rattling bone fragments, we planted his ashes in a green
eternity, palms flinging their locks against burnished cobalt     out
     past the church gate, a curious goat roped to a stake at the dirt
crossroads, the pastel ice cream concrete softening toward siesta, fronds
lolling on the moist air     uncle roger's spirit could choose to rest or
wander down one asphalt stretch and up another, gravel and dirt, until he
reach the ocean, lime     read the extended lines of cursive foaming on
brown, surging to shore, double-spaced     phalanxes of diaphanous prose

the palimpsest of the prairie          its bearded wheatgrass might have
nodded to the rhythm of the king james          wind's transparent wave riding
blonde grass, invisible ink sweeping over the recursive curve, no detail of my
life written in the narrows between the blades          i never cared to be a
pastoral poet, or a poet of small flatland longings, a poet of evangelical strictures,
of social discredit, fire and brimstone apoplexies          but of equatorial
revolutions, oceanic futures written in the veins of the vegetal
          tenements of babel dense with voices, languages spilling out the summer
windows onto the basketball-drubbed asphalt of little burgundy, montréal
the palimpsest city, one game played over another, one culture settled over
another, english spoken over créole spoken over french over each tenant a
turned page in each apartment, each apartment the idea of an island,
repeating upward 20 storeys, créole meltdowns simmering, pepperpot
sweating in those horizontal tenements that stacked and shipped my
ancestors across to islands, to new south american savannahs, new rivers,
new langugaes, new words fluttering in the mouth

turbulence in a blue tango jet, buffeted by cloud, engines roaming in stereo, pursuing the logic of better mus come        landing on this denuded, sparkling hinterland, flat slab of earth, before driving the long expressway in from the airport, crossing the bow river waiting in line for culture, another year
            barely inching forward. in the semi-basement barbershop in a northeast strip mall, low rent drop-ceiling and no cash register, next to speedy muffler, listening to dated dancehall hits, beenie man's slack stammer-simmer, thinking man this is fucking nowhere, prairie nowhere, terminal starlight tour, is this a beginning or a layover or

turning back, is this a beginning?　　　is it preferable to be erased, to have a
voice that does not know the chorus because it sounds outside the tradition,
because it is stolen by the chinook, or to have a dream of sweating in the
malarial mud swarmed by *morpho peleides*, sapphire butterflies, each one the
spirit of an ancestor　　　　is it better to own a new bungalow in a
new development, or to live where your name was born, where your memory
has tongue　　　is this the reckoning: being between, turning between a
newness of mr. clean and president's choice, and choke-and-rob in the bloody
dusk, between a full tank of gas and love in a time of bauxite strikes　　　i have
to reckon with this far reach, this far flung, this beyond beyond the
perimeter, wandering latitudes of longing and ache, where there exists no
critical authentic, no mas, nothing but blown fragments, and a polaroid
　　　frozen at the departure gate, timehri in 1973.　　　i look up from my
aunt's afro.　　　out the sedan's window: mile markers, flashing fenceposts and
barb wire slung between

clouds, unconscious in their blind dreaming     the prairies stretch beyond
death, baffle the compass          earthen tongues ripple speechless under dead
air, weightless volume of big sky          the foothills, humpbacked brown
leviathan, surface and plunge          a volcanic hollow     *une coulée de*
*pensées, une coulée de lettres, une coulée de lave*          the athabasca glacier
recedes into prehistory, dinosaur ice trickling into time's crystalline wink
          reception weakening the further we          from the city, clear static
between stations, mountains as ancestors, blue teeth to the sun
          history the complex of freedom and catastrophe, the found, the
concrete, the territory          on the prairies the lanes move          the lines shift,
narrative swerves under cloud changing shape like a thought          i am the
merest vehicle, great engine of tongues babbling toward a still point          a giant
period blackly riding the hills' humped complexities, patterns beneath the
formulaic speech          the attempt to unite landscape and immortality
          talking to defeat direction          the pleasure of departure          the
vexation of return          the road like a dream, out of the dark into the
struggle          the new morning so barren          furious outsider wandering
the edge of the river valley          the whooping cranes that mate for life
          the tyranny of this stolen narrative          the fields of grain shift

# THE POETS

ABIGAIL CHABITNOY earned her M.F.A. in poetry at Colorado State University and was a 2016 Peripheral Poets fellow. Her poems have appeared in *Hayden's Ferry Review*, *Boston Review*, *Tin House*, *Gulf Coast*, *LitHub*, and *Red Ink*, among others. She is a Koniag descendant and member of the Tangirnaq Native Village in Kodiak, Alaska, grew up in Pennsylvania, and currently resides in Colorado. *How to Dress a Fish* is her debut poetry collection.

SHARON OLDS was born in San Francisco and educated at Stanford University and Columbia University. The winner of both the Pulitzer Prize and England's T. S. Eliot Prize for her 2012 collection, *Stag's Leap*, she is the author of eleven previous books of poetry and the winner of many other honours, including the National Book Critics Circle Award for *The Dead and the Living*. Olds teaches in the Graduate Creative Writing Program at New York University and helped found the NYU outreach programs, among them the writing workshop for residents of Goldwater Hospital on Roosevelt Island, and for the veterans of the Iraq and Afghanistan wars. She lives in New York City.

SARAH RIGGS is the author of five books of poetry in English: *Waterwork* (2007), *Chain of Miniscule Decisions in the Form of a Feeling* (2007), *60 Textos* (2010), *Autobiography of Envelopes* (2012), and *Pomme & Granite* (2015). She has translated and co-translated six books of contemporary French poetry into English, including most recently Oscarine Bosquet's *Present Participle*. She lives in Brooklyn, NY.

ETEL ADNAN was born in Beirut, Lebanon, in 1925. She studied philosophy at the Sorbonne, UC Berkeley, and Harvard, and taught at Dominican College in San Rafael, California. In 2014 she was awarded one of France's highest cultural honours: l'Ordre de Chevalier des Arts et des Lettres, and she was a winner of the Lambda Literary Award for Lesbian Poetry and the California Book Award for Poetry, in 2013, for *Sea and Fog*. Her most recent books are *Night* (2016) and *Surge* (2018).

NATALIE SCENTERS-ZAPICO is a *fronteriza* from the sister cities of El Paso, Texas, U.S., and Ciudad Juárez, Chihuahua, México. Her first collection, *The Verging Cities* (2015), won the PEN America/ Joyce Osterweil Award, GLCA's New Writers Award, NACCS Foco Book Prize, and Utah Book Award. *Lima :: Limón* is her second collection. She has won fellowships from the Lannan Foundation, CantoMundo, and a Ruth Lilly and Dorothy Sargent Rosenberg Fellowship from the Poetry Foundation. Her poems have appeared in a wide range of anthologies and literary magazines, including *Best American Poetry 2015*, *POETRY*, *Tin House*, *Kenyon Review*, and more. She is currently teaching at the University of Puget Sound in Tacoma, Washington, U.S.

CHANTAL GIBSON is an artist-educator living in Vancouver with ancestral roots in Nova Scotia. Her visual art collection *Historical In(ter)ventions*, a series of altered history book sculptures, dismantles text to highlight language as a colonial mechanism of oppression. *How She Read* is another altered book, a genre-blurring extension of her artistic practice. Sculpting black text against a white page, her poems forge new spaces that challenge historic representations of Black womanhood and Otherness in the Canadian cultural imagination. *How She Read* is Gibson's debut book of poetry. An award-winning teacher, she teaches writing and visual communication in the School of Interactive Arts & Technology at Simon Fraser University.

DOYALI ISLAM's poems have been published in *Kenyon Review Online*, *The Fiddlehead*, and *The Best Canadian Poetry in English*, and have won several national contests and prizes. Doyali serves as the poetry editor of *Arc Poetry Magazine*. In 2017 she was a guest on CBC Radio's *The Sunday Edition*, and she was a poetry finalist for the National Magazine Awards. She lives in Toronto, Ontario. *heft* is her second collection of poetry.

KAIE KELLOUGH is a novelist, poet, and sound performer. He was born in Vancouver, British Columbia, raised in Calgary, Alberta, and in 1998 moved to Montreal, Quebec, where he now lives. He is the author of the novels *Dominoes at the Crossroads* and *Accordéon*, which was a finalist for the Amazon.ca First Novel Award; two books of poetry, *Lettricity* and *Maple Leaf Rag*; and two albums, *Vox:Versus* and *Creole Continuum*. He has performed and published internationally.

# THE JUDGES

PAULA MEEHAN was born in Dublin, where she still lives. She studied at Trinity College, Dublin, and at Eastern Washington University in the U.S. She has published seven collections of poetry, which have received both popular and critical acclaim. She has moderated workshops in the community, in prisons, in recovery programs, and has worked extensively with emerging poets inside and outside universities. Her work has been translated into French, German, Galician, Italian, Japanese, Estonian, Portuguese, Spanish, Greek, Chinese, and Irish. She has received the Butler Literary Award for Poetry presented by the Irish American Cultural Institute, the Marten Toonder Award for Literature, the Denis Devlin Award for *Dharmakaya*, published in 2000, the Lawrence O'Shaughnessy Award for Poetry 2015, and the PPI Award for Radio Drama. Dedalus Press has published *Mysteries of the Home*, a selection of seminal poems from the 1980s and the 1990s. She was honoured with election to Aosdána, the Irish Academy for the Arts, in 1996. She was Ireland Professor of Poetry, 2013–2016, and her public lectures from these years, *Imaginary Bonnets with Real Bees in Them*, was published by UCD Press in 2016. *Geomantic*, her latest collection of poems, was published by Dedalus Press, Dublin, in 2016 and received a Cholmondeley Award.

KEI MILLER was born in Jamaica in 1978 and has written several books across a range of genres. His 2014 collection, *The Cartographer Tries to Map a Way to Zion*, won the Forward Prize for Best Collection, while his 2017 novel, *Augustown*, won the Bocas Prize for Caribbean Literature, the Prix Les Afriques, and the Prix Carbet de la Caraïbe et du Tout-Monde. He is also an essayist. In 2010, the Institute of Jamaica awarded him the Silver Musgrave medal for his contributions to literature, and in 2018 he was awarded the Anthony Sabga medal for Arts & Letters. Kei has an M.A. in Creative Writing from Manchester Metropolitan University and a Ph.D. in English Literature from the University of Glasgow. He has taught at the Universities of Glasgow, Royal Holloway, and Exeter. He is the 2019 Ida Beam Distinguished Visiting Professor to the University of Iowa and is a Fellow of the Royal Society of Literature.

HOA NGUYEN is the author of several books of poetry, including *As Long as Trees Last*, *Red Juice*, and *Violet Energy Ingots*, which was shortlisted for the 2017 Griffin Poetry Prize. As a public proponent and advocate of contemporary poetry, she has served as guest editor for *The Best Canadian Poetry in English 2018* and she has performed and lectured at numerous institutions, including Princeton University, Bard College, Poet's House, and the Banff Centre's Writing Studio. The recipient of a 2019 Pushcart Prize and a 2020 Neustadt International Prize for Literature nomination, she has received grants and fellowships from the Canada Council for the Arts, the Ontario Arts Council, the MacDowell Colony, and the Millay Colony for the Arts. Her writing has garnered attention from such outlets as the *PBS News Hour*, *Granta*, *The Walrus*, *New York Times*, and *Poetry*, among others. Born in the Mekong Delta and raised and educated in the United States, Nguyen has lived in Canada since 2011.

# ACKNOWLEDGEMENTS

The publisher thanks the following for their kind permission to reprint the work contained in this volume:

"Family Ghosts," "[(   )]," "[*Grandfather*, fig. 2]," "[fig. 3]," "[fig.]," "[(shark)]," "[Not even bone.]," "[fig. with ghosts]," and "[(That's not how) the one from the water survived]" from *How to Dress a Fish* by Abigail Chabitnoy are reprinted by permission of Wesleyan University Press.

"My Father's Whiteness," "Hyacinth Aria," "I Cannot Say I Did Not," "From the Window of My Home-Town Hotel," "Her Birthday as Ashes in Seawater," and "When You Were First Visible" from *Arias* by Sharon Olds are reprinted by permission of Jonathan Cape and Alfred A. Knopf.

Excerpts from "October 27, 2003," "No Sky," and "Baalbeck," from *Time* by Etel Adnan, translated by Sarah Riggs, are reprinted by permission of Nightboat Books.

"He Has an Oral Fixation," "I Didn't Know You Could Buy," "She Is à la Mode," "Ixmiquilpan, Hidalgo, México," "Marianismo," and "Buen Esqueleto" from *Lima :: Limón* by Natalie Scenters-Zapico are reprinted by permission of Copper Canyon Press.

"homographs," "homonyms," "An Introduction to Cultural Studies," and "Mountain Pine Beetle Suite" from *How She Read* by Chantal Gibson are reprinted by permission of Caitlin Press.

"poem for your pocket," "visit to a thrift shop," "confronting global change," "the ant," "moving," "– 36th parallel –," and "daniel" from *heft* by Doyali Islam are reprinted by permission of McClelland & Stewart.

"keieteur falls" and excerpts from "mantra of no return" and "zero degrees" from *Magnetic Equator* by Kaie Kellough are reprinted by permission of McClelland & Stewart.

# THE GRIFFIN POETRY PRIZE
## ANTHOLOGY 2020

The best books of poetry published in English internationally and in Canada are honoured each year with the $65,000 Griffin Poetry Prize, one of the world's most prestigious and richest international literary awards. Since 2001 this annual prize has acted as a tremendous spur to interest in and recognition of poetry, focusing worldwide attention on the formidable talent of poets writing in English and works in translation. And each year the editor of *The Griffin Poetry Prize Anthology* gathers the work of the extraordinary poets shortlisted for the awards and introduces us to some of the finest poems in their collections.

This year, editor and prize juror Hoa Nguyen's selections from the international shortlist include poems from Abigail Chabitnoy's *How to Dress a Fish* (Wesleyan University Press), Sharon Olds's *Arias* (Jonathan Cape and Alfred A. Knopf), Etel Adnan's *Time*, translated by Sarah Riggs (Nightboat Books), and Natalie Scenters-Zapico's *Lima :: Limón* (Copper Canyon Press). The selections from the Canadian shortlist include poems from Chantal Gibson's *How She Read* (Caitlin Press), Doyali Islam's *heft* (McClelland & Stewart), and Kaie Kellough's *Magnetic Equator* (McClelland & Stewart).

In choosing the 2020 shortlist, prize jurors Paula Meehan, Kei Miller, and Hoa Nguyen each read 572 books of poetry, from 14 countries, including 37 translations. The jurors also wrote the citations that introduce the seven poets' nominated works.

104